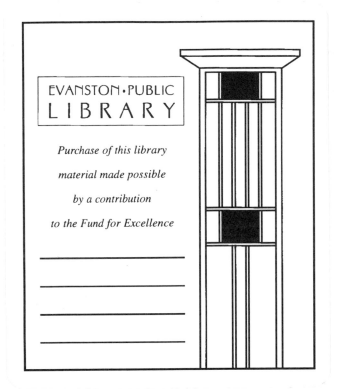

BLASTOFF!

THE SUN

BLASTOFF!

THE SUN

by Martin Schwabacher

BENCHMARK BOOKS

MARSHALL CAVENDISH

NEW YORK

WITH SPECIAL THANKS TO ROY A. GALLANT, PROFESSOR EMERITUS, SOUTHWESTERN PLANETARIUM, UNIVERSITY OF SOUTHERN MAINE, FOR HIS CAREFUL REVIEW OF THE MANUSCRIPT.

Benchmark Books
Marshall Cavendish
99 White Plains Road
Tarrytown, NY 10591-9001
www.marshallcavendish.com

Library of Congress Cataloging-in-Publication Data
Schwabacher, Martin.
The Sun / by Martin Schwabacher.
p. cm. — (Blastoff!)
Includes bibliographical references and index.
Summary: Discusses the shift from an Earth-centered to a Sun-centered view of the Solar System, the Sun's composition, history, and likely future, and the importance of this star to life on Earth.
ISBN 0-7614-1402-9
1. Sun—Juvenile literature. {1. Sun.] I. Title. II. Series.

QB521.5   .S32 2002   523.7-dc21

2001052410
Printed in Italy
1 3 5 6 4 2

Photo Research by Anne Burns Images
Cover Photo: © Frank Zullo/Photo Researchers Inc.

The photographs in this book are used by permission and through the courtesy of: Photo Researchers, 7; Jerry Schad, 9, 21; David Hardy/Science Photo Library, 15; William H. Mullins, 17; Omikron, 19; Michael Giannechini, 30; Lawrence Berkeley Lab/Science Photo Library, 33; Jisas/Lockheed/Science Photo Library, 37; R. Sanford, M. Agliolo, 42; B&C Alexander, 45; Frank Zullo, 49; Laguna Design/Science Photo Library, 51, 54; Julian Baum/Science Photo Library, 53; Scott Camazine/Superstock, 11, 43; The Cummer Museum of Art and Gardens, Jacksonville Bridgeman Art Library, 12; Fitzwilliam Museum, University of Cambridge Photo-Microstock, 22, 24, 25, 27, 29, 39, 46; NASA, 36.

CONTENTS

OUR NEIGHBORHOOD STAR

I t's easy to take the Sun for granted. All day, every day, it brings
light to the world, never taking a day off. But what is the Sun, really? Where did it come from, and what makes it glow so brightly?

The Sun is actually a star. It is not much different from the other
stars in the sky. The only reason it seems brighter than the other stars
is that it is much, much closer. The Sun is 260,000 times closer than
the next nearest star.

The Sun is just one of at least 200 billion stars in the Milky Way
galaxy, the cluster of stars we live in. The Milky Way, in turn, is just
one of 10 billion or more galaxies in the Universe. Seen from a planet
on the other side of the Milky Way, the Sun would look like just another
speck of light in the sky, a star like any other.

Though it is much closer than any other star, the Sun is still 93 million miles from Earth—far enough to make it appear much tinier than
it really is. It may look like a small, glowing ball, but the Sun is actually
109 times wider than Earth. Circling the Sun are nine planets, including
Earth, as well as thousands of smaller objects that together make the
Solar System. (Solar means having to do with the Sun.) The Sun is hundreds of times bigger than all the planets combined. In fact, about 99.8
percent of all the matter in the Solar System is contained in the Sun.

*The Sun is just one of billions of stars in the Milky Way galaxy. Many of the other
stars in the Milky Way can be seen in a band of stars spread across the night sky.*

The Kelvin Scale

The temperature on Earth is most often measured in degrees Fahrenheit (°F), or degrees Celsius (°C). But scientists often use another measurement to describe extreme temperatures, like those found in stars: units called Kelvin (K). Temperatures in the Kelvin scale equal the temperature in the Celsius scale plus 273 degrees. So, 0 °C = 273 K. Scientists prefer the Kelvin scale because there are no temperatures below zero in the Kelvin scale. On the Kelvin scale, zero degrees is known as absolute zero, because that is as cold as anything can get.

Like most stars, the Sun is made almost completely of hydrogen and helium, the two lightest gases in the Universe. By weight, the Sun is about 72 percent hydrogen and 27 percent helium. Small amounts of carbon, nitrogen, oxygen, nickel, gold, uranium, and other elements together make up about one percent of the total.

There is no solid surface on the Sun. There is nothing solid inside it either. It is just a giant ball of gas. But in the center the gas is squeezed so tightly that it is ten times as dense as gold.

The central core is where the Sun's tremendous heat is produced. There the hydrogen atoms are pressed together so hard that they explode, as if 100 billion hydrogen bombs were going off every second. These nonstop explosions heat the core to about 27,000,000 degrees

Thousands of objects, including Earth, orbit the Sun. Just inside the orbit of Jupiter, the fifth planet, is a ring of small, rocky asteroids. Now and then a comet swoops around the Sun on a long, narrow orbit.

Fahrenheit (about 15,000,000 °C).

The light and heat produced in the Sun are what keep us alive. Without this energy from the Sun, Earth would freeze, and all life on Earth would die. But the Sun won't burn out any time soon. The Sun has been glowing steadily for about 5 billion years, and it will keep doing so for another 5 billion.

2

CENTURIES OF SUNWATCHING

Before people had clocks or electric lights, the Sun told them when to get up and when to go to bed. Because most people worked outside on farms, instead of indoors in cities, they kept a close watch on the cycle of the seasons. In summer, the Sun rises higher and stays up longer than in winter. Days then start growing shorter, signaling that winter is coming. The shortest day of the year is called the Winter Solstice. This was traditionally a time of celebration in many parts of the world, because after the Winter Solstice the days grow longer, and spring returns.

Because life was so closely tied to the Sun's cycles, many people worshipped the Sun. To the Incas of South America, the Sun was the creator of the world. But to the Aztecs of Mexico, the Sun was the god of war, to whom they offered human sacrifices. The ancient Egyptians explained the daily disappearance of the Sun and its return the next morning with a story about their Sun god, Ra. Each night at sunset, Ra descended into the underworld, where he fought a terrible battle with Apep, the giant serpent of darkness. Only after he defeated the serpent could he rise again the next day.

At Stonehenge, in England, stands a ring of giant rocks erected thousands of years ago. The rocks form a pattern lining up with important points on the horizon, such as the place the Sun sets on the longest and shortest days of the year. Stonehenge might have been a giant calendar so accurate it could be used to predict eclipses.

Many religions have compared the setting and rising of the Sun, and the cycle of the seasons, to death and rebirth. This picture of the Egyptian Sun god, Ra, was painted on the coffin of Nespawershifi, an Egyptian ruler who died in 969 B.C. Ra had the head of a hawk and was usually shown with a disk representing the Sun.

In many places, the Sun represented the afterlife, or life after death. Its disappearance each night and return the next day are like a daily rebirth. And its return to full strength in the spring, after weakening each winter, is also like being reborn. Around 3300 B.C. in Newgrange, Ireland, ancient people built a huge tomb. Under a mound covered with carved stones and sparkling quartz, a long passage leads to a burial chamber where the builders put a basin containing the ashes of their dead. On the Winter Solstice, a shaft of light shines through a slot over the door and falls directly on the center of the burial chamber sixty-two feet away. Since this is the day the Sun begins its return to summer brightness, they may have hoped the souls of their dead relatives would also experience new life.

An even more dramatic structure is the famous circle of stones in England called Stonehenge. If you stand in the center of this ring of giant rocks and look through the center opening, a large stone about 250 feet (76 m) away marks the point where the Sun rises on the Summer Solstice, the longest day of the year. Other rocks point to where the Sun rises at the Winter Solstice and the spring and autumn equinoxes, when night and day are the same length.

Some consider Stonehenge a giant calendar so accurate it could be used to predict solar eclipses. These rare events occur when the Moon blocks our view of the Sun, causing all or part of the Sun to disappear. In the days when the Sun was considered a god, its disappearance could be very frightening. Eclipses were thought by some to occur when a giant snake started to eat the Sun, and observers danced and made loud noises to scare away the snake until the eclipse ended.

People who lived long ago also watched the Sun for practical reasons. In the southwestern United States, the Hopi people lived for generations by farming in the desert. To grow corn in such harsh, dry conditions, the seeds must be planted at exactly the right time: too early, and the last winter frosts will kill them; too late, and the corn will not have time to ripen. The Hopi knew exactly when to plant their seeds by using what are known as horizon calendars. These were precise drawings of the way the hills and landmarks look on the horizon. Each night, the Sun sets in a slightly different place. By

The Origin of Christmas

Many modern traditions go back to the days of Sun worship. Today's Christmas holiday started as a celebration of the Winter Solstice. Though it is now said to be the birthday of Jesus, no one really knows what day he was born. The Bible says nothing about the date, and historians think his real birthday was not even in winter. Christians did not start celebrating the birth of Jesus on December 25th until about 300 years after his death.

Before Jesus' birth, the Romans held a festival at the Winter Solstice called Saturnalia, during which they exchanged gifts. Some celebrated the Solstice as the birthday of Mithra, an ancient Persian god of light and wisdom. Around 600 years before Jesus, Mithra was combined with the Greeks' Sun god, Helios, and Mithra worship spread to Italy.

Long before Christ, worshippers of Mithra practiced baptism, communion, and the use of holy water, and observed Sunday as a holiday. They believed in humility, brotherly love, the immortal soul, and the resurrection, or death and rebirth, of their god. Though the Winter Solstice now occurs on either December 21 or 22, in the calendars used at the time, it fell on December 25. Christians attempted to win over the worshippers of Mithra by saying that their god was also born on December 25, and that Jesus was the true god of light and wisdom. This helped convert people who worshipped Mithra to Christianity.

On rare occasions, the Moon passes directly between Earth and the Sun, blocking part or all of the Sun from view. Seeing the Sun slowly disappear was a terrifying sight for people who did not know what was really happening.

always watching from a particular spot, observers could tell exactly what time of year it was by noting where the Sun set on the horizon. When it reached a particular hill, priests would announce that it was time to plant that year's crops.

SPINNING AROUND THE SUN

No matter where they lived, most ancient peoples agreed on two things: Earth stood still, and the Sun and stars circled around it. The heavenly bodies all rose in the east and set in the west, moving in giant circles, and Earth didn't move—that seemed obvious. Who can feel Earth moving?

In fact, both these commonsense observations are wrong. It may appear that the Sun rises and sets, but it is Earth that is moving, not the Sun. Look at it this way. Pretend your head is the Earth. Look at a lightbulb—that's the Sun. Now stand up and slowly turn in a circle. When your back is turned to the lightbulb, the Sun is out of sight, and it's night. Keep turning, and the Sun soon comes back into view— that's sunrise. When you're facing directly toward the lightbulb, the Sun is high in the sky, and it's noon. Keep turning, and the Sun will set.

One of the first people to figure out what was happening was the Greek astronomer Aristarchus. Around 250 B.C., he suggested that per- haps Earth is spinning, making the Sun and stars appear to move when they do not. He also was the first known person to suggest that Earth revolves around the Sun. But most people still thought Earth was the center of the Universe, and Aristarchus's ideas were not taken seriously for nearly two thousand years.

In the 1500s, Polish astronomer Nicolaus Copernicus put the Sun, rather than Earth, in the center of the Universe. This idea met with great resistance. One early supporter, Italian astronomer Galileo Galilei, was sentenced to house arrest by the Catholic Church for pub- lishing arguments that Copernicus was right.

Another believer in Copernicus's theory was German astronomer Johannes Kepler, who came up with mathematical laws that let him calculate the orbits of Earth and the other planets. Everything fell into place when English mathematician Sir Isaac Newton built on Kepler's laws of planetary motion and described his universal laws of gravitation.

Sir Isaac Newton (1642–1727) came up with a theory of gravity that explained why the planets orbit the Sun. Newton also figured out that sunlight is actually a blend of many different colors of light mixed together.

Newton's theories explained not only the orbits of the planets but why objects fall to the ground instead of floating off into space.

All matter attracts other matter with a force called gravity. The more matter an object contains, the stronger this force is. Gravity is what keeps you from falling off Earth. Earth is so massive that its gravity pulls you back down, no matter how hard you try to jump off. (Your body's gravity tugs back on Earth a little, too, but not enough to notice.)

The Sun is so massive that its gravity keeps the planets in orbit around it. Without the Sun's gravity, the planets would fly off into space. The planets tug back on the Sun, too, which makes the Sun wobble slightly. If you were looking at the Sun from outer space, you could observe it being pulled back and forth by the planets' gravity. Even if you were too far away to see the planets, you would still know they were there because of this motion. That is how the first planets outside the Solar System were found—not by seeing the planets themselves, but by seeing the effects of their gravity on the stars they orbit.

SIZING UP THE SUN

People have always wondered how far away the Sun is, and how big it is. Aristarchus tried to calculate its distance by measuring the angles of a giant triangle connecting Earth, the Sun, and the Moon. He concluded the Sun was twenty times farther away than the Moon. A better measurement came from Greek astronomer Hipparchus about 105 years later, around 150 B.C. He came up with a distance of 9 million miles (14 million km). This is still only one-tenth the actual distance, but it gave people an idea of how far away the Sun really is. To shine so brightly from such a vast distance, the Sun had to be many times bigger than Earth.

SUNWATCHERS

One of the hardest things about observing the Sun is that you can't look right at it. Staring at it can actually make you go blind. The damage can occur in two ways. Extremely bright light can trigger dangerous chemical reactions in the light-sensitive parts of your eyes. It can also heat up and literally cook the back of your eyes, causing blindness.

Telescopes only make this problem worse, because they make distant objects brighter. Making the Sun even brighter is very dangerous.

Rainbows appear when drops of water in the sky separate the different colors of light that together make up sunlight. In addition to all the colors of the rainbow, sunlight also contains invisible rays such as ultraviolet, infrared, radio waves, and X rays.

However, if you project a telescope image of the Sun on the wall, instead of looking directly at it, you can see details on the Sun you could never see with the naked eye.

One of the first people to observe the Sun through a telescope was Galileo. In 1610, he noticed that there were spots on the Sun. Galileo saw that the spots moved across the Sun's surface. By watching them from day to day, he discovered that the Sun was spinning, making a complete rotation about every twenty-six days.

SPLITTING SUNBEAMS

Another advance came from splitting sunlight into its different parts. Though sunlight looks yellowish white, it is actually a blend of many different colors of light. When you shine a sunbeam through a triangular piece of glass called a prism, the light spreads out into a wider beam showing all the colors of the rainbow. In fact, real rainbows are made much the same way, when ordinary sunlight is split apart by water droplets.

The rainbow created when light is spread out by a prism is called a spectrum. In the spectrum made by sunlight there are tiny dark stripes where particular colors are missing. In 1814, a German optician named Joseph von Fraunhofer began to study the lines in the solar spectrum with a new instrument called a spectroscope. Over the next few years, he carefully mapped 576 lines, which became known as Fraunhofer Lines. (There are about 25,000 of these lines in all.)

In 1859, two other Germans, Gustav Kirchhoff and Robert Bunsen, discovered that these lines showed what the Sun was made of. They found that heating chemicals in a flame produced bright lines along a color spectrum. Some of these bright lines matched up with Fraunhofer's dark lines. By identifying the pattern of lines produced by each chemical element, they could identify the chemical elements in the Sun.

The colors that make up sunlight can be separated into a rainbowlike spectrum by a prism. Particular chemicals absorb or emit specific colors of light, causing lines to appear in the solar spectrum.

Kirchhoff and Bunsen found lines for hydrogen, sodium, calcium, iron, and chromium, indicating that all of these existed in the Sun. But scientists were puzzled by a set of lines that matched no element known on Earth. They concluded that they had discovered a new element. They called it helium, after the Greek Sun god Helios. Only afterward was this gas discovered on Earth, trapped in pockets underground. It had never been discovered before because it floats upward—the reason it is now used to fill balloons.

Their discoveries indicated that the Sun was made of the same materials as Earth. Then an English physicist named Cecilia Payne calculated that hydrogen is a million times more abundant than iron in the Sun, and that helium—rare on Earth—was the second most abundant element. It seemed hard to believe that the Sun could be made mostly from these two light gases, but her calculations turned out to be correct.

Two astronauts repair the Solar Maximum *mission satellite in the cargo bay of the space shuttle* Challenger.

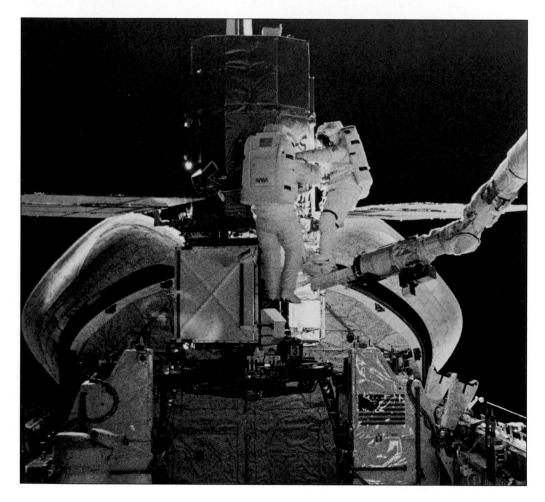

In the twentieth century, new instruments made it possible to detect invisible rays from the Sun. The visible light from the Sun creates a continuous spectrum with red on one end and violet on the other. But beyond violet, the spectrum continues with invisible ultraviolet rays, X rays, and gamma rays. At the red end, the spectrum continues with invisible infrared, microwaves, and radio waves.

It turns out that only 40 percent of the Sun's energy is released as visible light. The other 60 percent is released as these invisible rays. But the gamma rays, X rays, and most of the ultraviolet rays from the Sun never reach us because they are absorbed by our upper atmosphere. (This is fortunate, because even small amounts of these rays can cause cancer, and large amounts would make Earth uninhabitable.) Since most of these rays don't reach the ground, instruments had to be raised above Earth's atmosphere to measure them. This became possible with the development of space flight.

SUNWATCHING FROM SPACE

In 1980, the United States launched the *Solar Maximum* mission satellite into space. It was packed with instruments for measuring the Sun, including a special telescope for gathering gamma rays, which go right through ordinary mirrors. Instruments also measured the Sun's magnetic field, which is linked to sunspots.

In 1990, the *Ulysses* spacecraft was launched from the space shuttle *Discovery*. It traveled around the Sun, observing it from angles impossible on Earth. Earth's orbit loops around the middle of the Sun, but the *Ulysses* spacecraft traveled directly over the Sun's north and south poles. At the poles, the Sun's magnetic field is very different than at its equator. Data from *Ulysses* showed that particles streaming out of the Sun, called the solar wind, shoot out nearly twice as fast from the Sun's poles as from its equator.

The Solar and Heliospheric Observatory (SOHO), launched in

The SOHO spacecraft measures vibrations in the Sun's surface caused by sound waves traveling through the Sun. These waves cause the surface to rise and fall hundreds of feet per second and can create bulges several miles high.

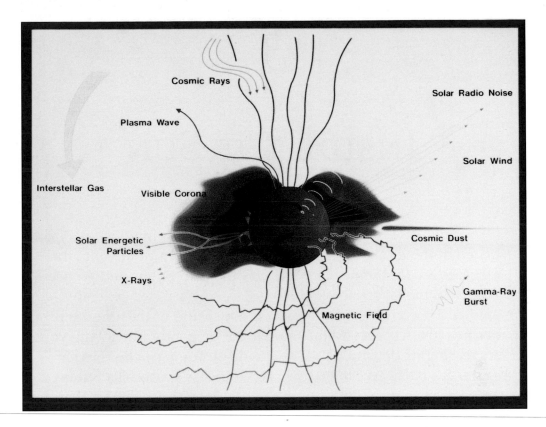

The Ulysses *spacecraft carries several instruments for measuring the Sun's emissions, including X rays, radio waves, gamma rays, and the particles blowing out in the solar wind.*

1995 by the European Space Agency and the National Aeronautics and Space Administration (NASA), has instruments that can measure what is happening deep inside the Sun. It detected rivers of gas flowing beneath the surface of the Sun, and vibrating pulses similar to sound waves bouncing around inside the Sun. These vibrations provide information about layers deep within the Sun that are otherwise hidden by the Sun's blazing surface.

3

INSIDE THE SUN

The Sun's hot gases can be divided into layers in which very different things are happening. In the outer part of the Sun, the gases are far thinner than the air on Earth. But as you go deeper into the Sun, the layers above press down, so the gases get compressed and become denser. Density is a measure of the amount of matter in a given space. If you squeeze cotton candy into a ball, you are increasing its density. Gases are made of tiny particles. Under pressure, gas particles can be squeezed into less space. The Sun's core is compressed so tightly it is more than thirteen times denser than lead and 150 times denser than water.

THE CORE

The pressure in the middle of the Sun is 300 million times greater than the air pressure on Earth. The core takes up just 1.6 percent of the Sun's total volume, but 40 percent of the Sun's matter is crammed into that space. When atoms are squeezed together, they heat up. In the nineteenth century, scientists thought squeezing caused by the Sun's gravity might account for the Sun's heat and light. This pressure

A false-color photo of the Sun showing the invisible ultraviolet light emitted from the inner corona. The dark patches at the Sun's north and south poles are coronal holes, where the solar wind blows out the fastest.

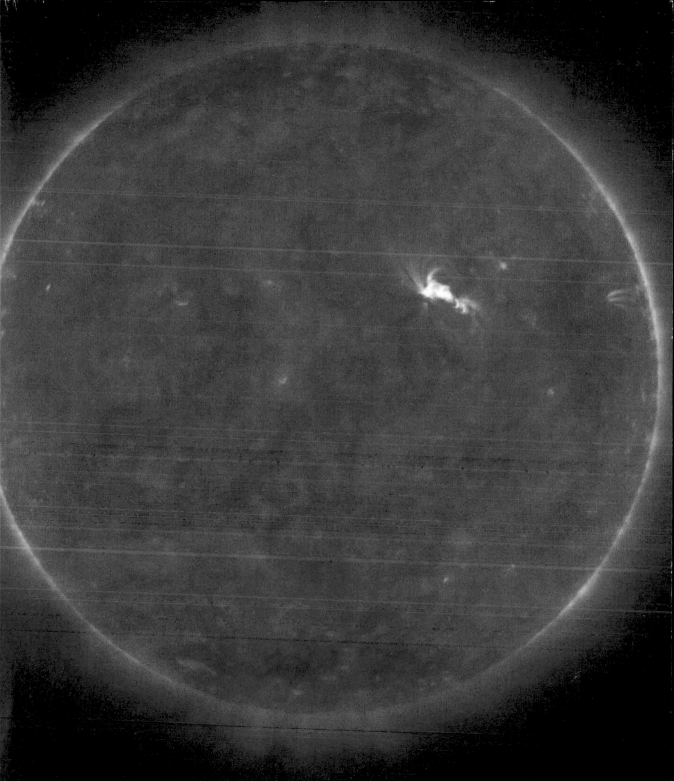

could in fact keep it glowing for about 30 million years. But the Sun has been glowing for 150 times that long. Clearly there had to be some other source for the Sun's energy. The answer turned out to be nuclear fusion—the same thing that powers atomic bombs.

NUCLEAR FUSION

When you burn wood or gasoline, heat is released by a chemical reaction. In a chemical reaction, the bonds connecting atoms break and reconnect like Tinkertoys, but the atoms themselves do not change. In a nuclear reaction, however, one kind of atom is actually changed into another. Nuclear reactions release far more energy than do chemical reactions.

All atoms have a center called a nucleus. The term *nuclear reaction* means involving the nucleus. The nucleus is made of protons and neutrons. Outside the nucleus are electrons. Hydrogen is the smallest kind of atom. Its nucleus contains just one proton and no neutrons. The second smallest is helium, with two protons and two neutrons.

In the Sun's core, the pressure is so great that hydrogen nuclei are stripped of their electrons. Matter in this state is neither a solid, liquid, or gas. It is called plasma. The nuclei of all atoms carry a positive electrical charge, which pushes away other nuclei. It takes enormous temperature and pressure to force two positively charged hydrogen nuclei together. But when this happens, they can stick together, or fuse, into a single nucleus. This is called nuclear fusion.

When four hydrogen nuclei fuse together, the result is a helium nucleus. It takes a series of several different reactions to accomplish this. In some, protons are changed into neutrons, and a great deal of energy is released. Each helium nucleus has 0.7 percent less mass than the four hydrogen nuclei that created it. This tiny amount of mass is converted into an immense amount of energy. According to Albert Einstein's famous equation, $E=mc^2$, the energy produced (E) is equal

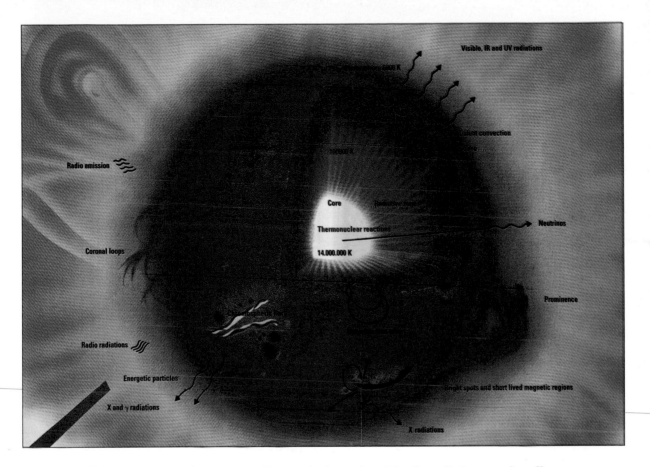

Visible, IR and UV radiations

Radio emission

100000 K

Core

Thermonuclear reactions

14.000.000 K

Neutrinos

Coronal loops

Prominence

Radio radiations

Energetic particles

Bright spots and short lived magnetic regions

X and γ radiations

X radiations

A diagram of the Sun's structure. The core is shown in white, the radiative zone in yellow, and the outer layers in orange.

to the amount of mass used up (m) times the speed of light squared (c²). This is a very large number.

Fusing one pound of hydrogen into helium releases as much energy as burning 6 million gallons (about 25 million l) of gasoline. In the core of the Sun, 700 million tons of hydrogen are converted to helium each second. Of this amount, 5 million tons are converted into pure energy. This is the source of the Sun's light and heat.

Part of a neutrino observatory that was buried more than 1 mile (2,115 meters) underground in Sudbury, Canada. About 10,000 photomultiplier tubes were attached to this framework to amplify the faint pulses of light emitted when invisible neutrinos strike the target material placed in the center.

SNAGGING NEUTRINOS

One of the by-products of nuclear fusion are tiny particles called neutrinos. Neutrinos are so small that scientists are not sure whether they contain any matter at all. Neutrinos go right through other matter with ease. Ten trillion neutrinos fly through your body every second. These neutrinos are created in the Sun.

Almost nothing can stop a neutrino, but scientists have managed to catch a few of them. They put a 100,000-gallon tank of tetrachloroethylene—normally used as a cleaning fluid—in an old gold mine in South Dakota. About every three days, a neutrino is captured and leaves its mark. This proved the Sun was creating neutrinos, but it also raised new questions because the fluid stopped less than half as many neutrinos as expected. Scientists are still trying to figure out what happened to the missing neutrinos.

THE RADIATIVE ZONE

The layer outside the Sun's core is called the radiative zone. It stretches from about a quarter of the way out from the center to about three-quarters of the way out. It is called the radiative zone because the energy created in the core must radiate through it to escape.

The gases in this zone are packed so tightly that light and heat have trouble passing through them. Near the top of the radiative zone the gases are thicker than water. Near the core, they are denser than cement.

As each bit of energy, or photon, created in the core hits an atom in the radiative zone, it is blocked and absorbed. The atom then spits out a new burst of energy, but in a different direction—perhaps backward, forward, or to the side. This new photon does not get far before being absorbed by another atom. The energy is released again, once more in a random direction. It is like a ball trapped in a giant pinball machine. Each ray of sunlight changes direction so many times that it takes an average of 170,000 years to escape the radiative zone. By blocking the escape of energy from the core, the radiative zone keeps the core hot enough to continue its nuclear reactions.

THE CONVECTIVE ZONE

Energy has an easier time moving outward in the next layer, the convective zone. Here, when a gas atom absorbs a photon of energy, it does not spit it back out. Instead, it simply heats up. The heated gas at the bottom of the convective zone rises to the surface, taking this energy with it. It reaches the upper boundary of the convective zone in a mere ten days, where it releases its energy to the next higher layer, which is very near the Sun's surface.

The cool gas then sinks back to the bottom of the convective zone, where it heats up and repeats the process. This cycle of rising and falling is called convection. You can see a similar thing happening inside a Lava Lamp, as the oozing liquid is heated from the bottom. It rises, cools, and falls again, in an endless cycle of convection.

The pockets of gas that rise and fall within the convective zone are called cells. Each cell is as big as Earth. Smaller cells called granules swirl at the surface. Granules last only a few minutes. As brightly colored, hotter cells arise next to darker, cooler ones, they create a checkerboard pattern of light and dark spots.

THE PHOTOSPHERE

Atop the convective zone is a thin layer, barely 300 miles (483 km) thick, called the photosphere. Its gases are about as dense as our air at sea level. It is named for the Greek word for light, *photos*, because it is where the sunlight finally escapes and beams out into space.

The Sun's Surface

The photosphere is considered the surface of the Sun, but this is misleading, because there really is no surface on the Sun, as there is on Earth. Earth's surface is where the solid ground or liquid ocean ends, and the gas atmosphere begins. But the boundary between the surface and the atmosphere on the Sun is really just an imaginary line between thicker and thinner gases.

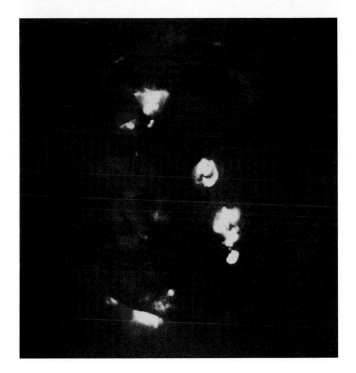

This X-ray image of the Sun taken by the YOHKOH *satellite shows the activity of the corona, the outer layer of the solar atmosphere.*

The farther out from the core, the thinner the Sun's gases are. The gases in the convective layer are too dense to let light pass through—that is why they heat up and rise. The photosphere is the first layer thin enough to be transparent. Since the photosphere lets energy pass through, rather than absorbing it and heating up, its temperature drops to 5,780 K, compared to 2,200,000 K at the base of the convective zone.

THE SUN'S ATMOSPHERE

Above the photosphere is a layer of gas called the chromosphere. It is considered part of the Sun's atmosphere because the gas there is so thin you can see right through it, unlike the denser and brighter inner layers. When the rest of the Sun is blocked from view, as during an

MYSTERIOUS HEATING

One of the greatest mysteries about the Sun is why the gases in the corona have a higher temperature than those in the chromosphere, even though the corona is farther from the Sun's heat-producing core. Though the chromosphere is barely 50,000 K, the corona can reach a temperature of 2,000,000 K. Usually when things move away from a heat source, they cool down. Yet in the corona, gases get hotter as they move *away* from the Sun.

One explanation is that energy is transferred to the corona by magnetic fields, and is then converted to heat. Photos of the corona often show loops of gas that bulge out of the Sun and curl back in. These loops are shaped by magnetic fields. When these loops snap, they can instantly heat the gases in the corona by a million degrees.

eclipse, you can see the chromosphere glowing pink or red, which is why it is named for the Greek word for color, *chromos*. The gases in the outer chromosphere are ten trillion times thinner than the air on Earth.

Beyond the chromosphere is the corona, from the Latin for *crown*. These wispy strands can stretch as far as the entire width of the Sun. Though the corona glows dimly, it is only one-millionth as bright as the photosphere. The corona is too dim to see in daylight. However, if the rest of the Sun is blocked by an eclipse, or by a dark circle in an instrument called a coronagraph, the corona's crownlike rays can be seen.

THE ACTIVE SUN

Particles that stream out of the Sun's corona are called the solar wind. These particles blow all the way to Earth and beyond. Because the Sun does not shine steadily, but has huge storms on its billowing surface, the solar wind sometimes comes in big gusts.

A major source of the stormy weather on the Sun is its magnetic field. Magnetism is a force that, like gravity, can push or pull on things without touching them.

Magnetism is related to electricity. The Sun contains many trillions of tons of moving electrons and electrically charged particles called ions. This motion creates an intense magnetic field. Since the movement of the ions inside the Sun is not constant and steady, neither is the Sun's magnetic field.

Areas of strong magnetic fields are what cause sunspots. Sunspots are dark patches on the Sun's surface. They occur when strong magnetic fields block the flow of heat from the Sun. Sunspots are thousands of degrees cooler than the surrounding areas, which makes them less bright.

SUNSPOTS AND FLARES

Sunspots usually occur in pairs. The two spots are connected by a magnetic field that loops out from the Sun and back in. Sometimes these looping magnetic fields touch, and the immense energy they contain is instantly freed, like a rubber band snapping.

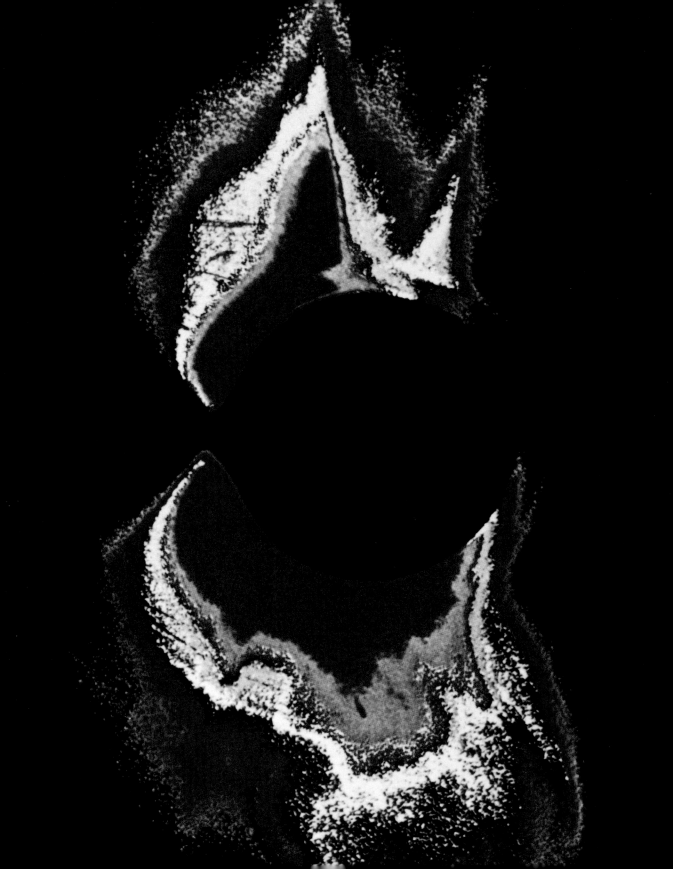

Sudden bursts of energy and ions frequently flare out from the Sun. Prominences and flares may occur when loops of magnetic fields suddenly snap.

When this happens, a burst of energy called a solar flare shoots out of the Sun. These massive explosions release as much energy as a billion atomic bombs and can heat an area the size of Earth by more than 10 million degrees in minutes. Since most of the energy released is in the form of X rays and radio waves, you can't see flares. But if you could see X rays the way you can see light, a flare would outshine the entire rest of the Sun.

Another huge explosion caused by the Sun's changing magnetic fields is called a coronal mass ejection (CME). But instead of just shooting out energy like a flare, CMEs eject billions of tons of matter out into space. When these particles reach Earth, they can cause northern lights, ion storms, and other strange effects described in the next chapter.

Left: Particles streaming out from the Sun blow all the way to Earth and beyond. This solar wind can damage satellites and interfere with radio and electrical systems on Earth.

4

FROM SUN TO EARTH

Just 0.000000000005 percent of the Sun's energy reaches Earth—less than a trillionth of its total radiation. But this is enough to keep our planet warm and livable. Without this sunlight, all the water on Earth would freeze, and everything would die.

The amount of sunlight reaching Earth changes a little from day to day and year to year, but these changes are slight—just a fraction of a percent. On the whole, the solar energy reaching Earth averages 127 watts per square foot (1,368 watts per square meter). This is roughly equivalent to two 60-watt lightbulbs shining over every one-foot-square patch of sky, or twenty-three bulbs per square meter. Though clouds sometimes keep some of this light from reaching the ground, the amount that reaches the upper atmosphere always stays close to this number, which is called the solar constant.

The Sun's ultraviolet radiation varies ten times as much as the sunlight you can see, and its X-ray emissions are a hundred times more variable. During peak emissions, the extra radiation can cause the temperature in the upper atmosphere to double, because that is where these rays are absorbed.

Though clouds prevent some sunlight from reaching the ground, the total amount of sunlight that reaches Earth's atmosphere is always fairly constant.

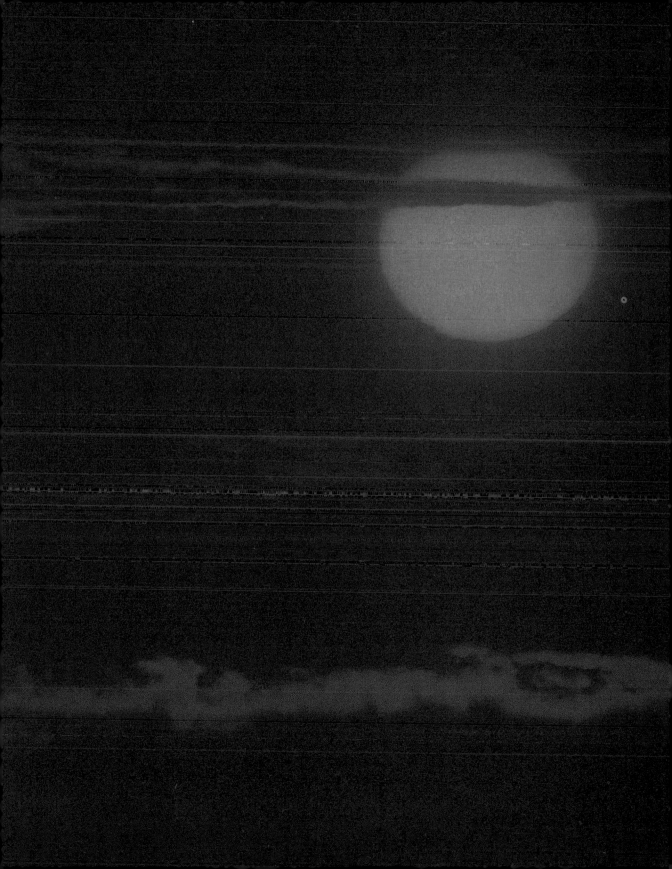

THE SOLAR CYCLE

One of the strangest things about the Sun is that sunspots, flares, and coronal mass ejections are not steady from year to year, but increase and decrease according to a regular pattern, or cycle. Every eleven years, the number of sunspots rises to a peak. This period is called the solar maximum. Halfway in between these peaks, at the solar minimum, sunspots are much rarer.

Though sunspots are cooler than the rest of the photosphere, the Sun actually glows hotter, not cooler, when there are more sunspots. This is because the intense magnetic activity that causes sunspots also causes more high-temperature emissions such as flares and coronal mass ejections.

SPACE WEATHER

Though you won't feel any warmer during a solar maximum, you may hear more static on your radio. Electrons, protons, and other ions stream out of the Sun all the time. Storms on the Sun can send huge gusts of these electrically charged particles shooting toward Earth. Ions striking Earth's magnetic field can generate radio waves, which interfere with radio signals and communication satellites.

A blast of ions from the Sun can also cause Earth's magnetic field to change shape. When any magnetic field moves, it generates an electric current. A change in Earth's magnetic field can cause electricity to surge through power lines. In 1989—near a solar maximum—a huge ion storm caused a power surge so strong that it shut down the electrical system in Quebec, Canada, stopping the Montreal subway from running and closing many businesses.

A more pleasant effect of ions from the Sun are beautiful, wavy lines of light in the night sky called northern or southern lights, or auroras. They are created when ions strike atoms in the atmosphere,

THE SOURCE OF
THE SOLAR CYCLE

Though people have observed the sunspot cycle since the 1840s, its cause is still not well understood. But satellite measurements have recently revealed things happening inside the Sun that could be affecting its magnetic field and causing the solar cycle.

Because the Sun does not have a solid surface, different parts can rotate at different speeds. The Sun's surface spins fastest at the equator, making one complete rotation every 25.4 days. Near the poles, however, the Sun's surface rotates once every 33 days.

Down below, in the radiative zone, the gases spin as a solid ball. But above, in the convective zone, they rotate at different rates. So, at the boundary between the radiative zone and the convective zone, layers of gas moving at greatly different speeds rub against each other. Any movement of electrically charged particles creates a magnetic field—so the swirling and mixing between these layers affect the Sun's magnetic field. Layers rotating at different speeds could cause regular peaks in magnetic activity in much the same way that the hour hand and the minute hand on a clock line up at regular intervals.

Northern lights, or auroras, in Manitoba, Canada. Auroras appear when electrically charged ions from the Sun strike atoms in Earth's atmosphere, causing them to glow. Because Earth's magnetic field guides these ions toward the north and south poles, auroras are brightest near the poles.

causing them to glow. They are brightest in the far north and far south, because Earth's magnetic field channels ions from the Sun toward the poles, where they stream down through the sky. Auroras can occur anytime, but they are brightest during a solar maximum. In 2000, near the peak of the solar cycle, auroras could be seen as far south as North Carolina.

SUNSPOTS AND CLIMATE

At solar maximum, the slightly higher amount of energy reaching Earth might cause slightly higher global temperatures, but another solar cycle could have a much more significant effect on climate. Over longer time periods, there are gaps in the solar cycle. From 1645 to 1715, for example, astronomers noted that sunspots virtually disap-

Variations in the solar cycle may change the climate on Earth. Some people believe reduced solar activity from 1645 to 1715 might have caused a period of extremely cold weather known as the Little Ice Age. This painting from that period, titled Canal in Winter, *is by Dutch artist Klaese Molenaer.*

peared. During this seventy-year period, Earth's climate was much colder than average—so cold that the era became known as the Little Ice Age. It is possible that the unusual climate was caused by the change in solar activity. In fact, scientists have shown that the four major ice ages of the past four thousand years all occurred during periods of reduced solar activity. This could point to a link between the solar cycle and the climate.

SPACE WEATHER AND HEALTH

Radiation from the Sun can endanger human health. Though the most dangerous rays, such as gamma rays and X rays, are absorbed by the air before they reach the ground, it is possible that people who travel frequently by airplane could be exposed to unhealthy doses. Repeated exposure could pose a special risk to pilots and flight attendants. Scientists may start advising travelers to be careful during the solar maximum, and even suggest postponing travel when an ion storm approaches. Especially dangerous is flying near the North Pole, because much of the solar wind is channeled there by Earth's magnetic field.

Even down on the ground, sunshine can affect human health. Not all of the Sun's ultraviolet light is blocked in the upper atmosphere. The ultraviolet (UV) light in sunshine is what causes your skin to tan, and sometimes burn. Ultraviolet rays also cause skin cancer, especially in people who tan themselves excessively. That is why scientists are so concerned about the chemical pollution that damages the ozone layer. Ozone is a form of oxygen that blocks UV light in the upper atmosphere. Chemicals called chlorofluorocarbons, which are used in air conditioners and many other products, float up to the ozone layer and destroy enough ozone to let more UV through. They are being phased out, but people all over the world suffer increased risk of skin cancer from past pollution.

Sunspots seen from the Kitt Peak National Observatory in Arizona. The number of sunspots changes from year to year according to an eleven-year cycle.

All life on Earth relies on energy from the Sun. Plants use the energy in sunlight to grow, in a process called photosynthesis. These sunflowers grow so large and are so hardy because they thrive under the sun's rays.

Of course, sunlight usually does more good than harm. Sunlight on your skin produces vitamin D, which is essential for human health. And during winter, when there is less daylight, many people get depressed, indicating that sunlight is good for the emotions, too.

FUELED BY THE SUN

Another way we rely on the Sun's energy is in food production. All plants contain stored solar energy in the form of sugar and other molecules. This is why eating plant products gives our bodies energy. Even the energy we get from eating meat comes indirectly from the Sun, because the animals we eat for meat grow by eating plants. Other sources of energy, including the gasoline that powers your car, the oil or natural gas that heats your home, and the coal used in electrical power plants, were all produced by ancient plant life. So the energy in your food, your car, and your television can all be traced back to the energy released when hydrogen is turned into helium inside the Sun.

5

THE LIFE AND DEATH OF THE SUN

All life on Earth depends on the Sun. So, what would happen if the Sun went out? What does the future hold in store for the Sun? To understand where the Sun is headed, it helps to understand where it came from.

According to current theories, it all started with the Big Bang. About 15 billion years ago, the Universe did not exist. All the matter and energy that now make up the stars, planets, and your body were once contained in a single point, called a singularity. For some unknown reason, the singularity suddenly exploded, giving rise to the first atoms in the Universe—hydrogen nuclei, which consist of a single proton. Some of these protons then fused to become helium nuclei, just as they do inside the Sun and other stars today. Just a few seconds after the Big Bang the atomic particles had spread so far apart that this fusion reaction stopped. Nine-tenths of the atoms in the Universe were now hydrogen, and the rest helium. No other chemical elements existed. Bigger atoms, like the ones in your body and in the ground beneath your feet, were all made later, inside stars.

According to the Big Bang theory, all the matter in the Universe was once contained in a single point called a singularity. About 15 billion years ago, this singularity exploded. All the particles that would later form the stars and planets came shooting outward.

THE FAMILY OF STARS

Stars formed when clouds of small particles were pulled together by the force of gravity. There are several different kinds of stars, depending on the amount of matter in the cloud, or nebula, they started from. The smallest stars never get hot enough for fusion to start. They just glow faintly from the heat in their compressed centers. These are called Brown Dwarfs. Stars that are barely large enough to cause fusion in their cores are called Red Dwarfs. Next brightest are the Main Sequence stars, like the Sun, which glow a bright yellow. Brighter yet are the Blue and White Giants. These stars can be hundreds of times larger and thousands of times brighter than the Sun. Some supergiants are so big they could contain a billion Suns.

EXPLODING SUPERGIANTS

The centers of the largest stars are so hot that, through nuclear fusion, they can create much bigger atoms than helium. Iron, for example, has twenty-six protons and thirty neutrons in its nucleus. Only the hottest stars can fuse that many protons together.

Atoms bigger than iron, however, are created only when giant stars explode. These explosions, called supernovas, blaze hundreds of millions of times brighter than the Sun in blasts that last for weeks. In the past few thousand years, only a handful of supernovas have been seen from Earth. In 1054, Chinese astronomers saw what seemed to be a new star suddenly appear in the sky. It glowed so brightly that it could be seen during broad daylight. Today, the remains of this exploded star can be seen through a telescope. The expanding cloud of gas is called the Crab Nebula.

Supernovas release more energy in a few seconds than the brightest stars do in hundreds of thousands of years. The heaviest elements in the Universe, including gold, silver, and uranium, are formed in

An artist's illustration shows Blue and White Giants forming from a nebula of hydrogen gas. At the end of their lives, these large stars will explode in giant supernovas.

supernovas or in giant explosions created when stars collide. After these explosions, expanding clouds of dust and gas carry the newly formed atoms across the Universe. We know that at least one such cloud of gas reached us because we can see the evidence right here on Earth. Every ounce of gold on our planet, as well as many of the atoms in your body, originally came from a supernova trillions of miles away.

A STAR IS BORN

When this blast of supernova gas reached our area, the Sun had not yet formed; it was still a nebula of dust and gas. It is possible that the pressure of the supernova cloud hitting the solar nebula may be what triggered its collapse into a ball, and thus helped to form our Sun.

Before this collapse, our nebula was spinning slowly. As gravity pulled it inward, it sped up, and the spinning gas formed a flat disk. The outer part of this flat disk collected into blobs that became planets. The inner area formed the Sun.

Until it was compacted tightly enough for fusion to start, the ball of gas glowed red from heat caused by compression. This glowing ball is called a protostar (*proto* means before). About 4.5 billion years ago, when the protostar's center reached about 10 million K, fusion started. The Sun had become a star.

THE TEMPERATURE'S RISING

Since then, the Sun has burned more or less steadily. The heat in its core creates pressure that pushes the Sun's gases outward. But at the same time, gravity is pulling the surface gases back down. The balance between the two prevents any sudden changes.

The Sun has been changing gradually, however, since its birth. When its fusion furnace first ignited, the Sun was only 70 percent as

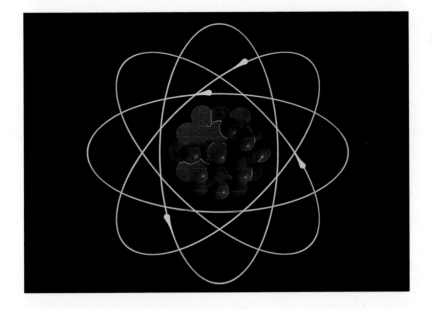

All atoms contain a center, or nucleus, of protons and neutrons (shown here as blue and yellow dots) surrounded by electrons. The nucleus of the smallest atom, hydrogen, contains a single proton. Immediately after the Big Bang these were the only atoms in the Universe. All the larger atoms formed from nuclear fusion, in which the nuclei of smaller atoms collide and join together.

bright as it is now. As the hydrogen in its core was consumed, the core shrank, which caused it to heat up. This heat caused the Sun to glow brighter and hotter, which made it expand. In fact, the Sun is now 6 percent wider than it was 4.5 billion years ago.

Even though the Sun has been "burning" hydrogen for 4.5 billion years, it has consumed less than one percent of its total material. But it has used up 37 percent of the hydrogen fuel in its core. In 5 to 7 billion years, the remaining usable hydrogen in the core will be gone.

By that time, however, Earth will already have been burned to a crisp. As the Sun uses up its hydrogen, it will continue to expand and grow hotter. In 3 billion years the Sun will be hot enough to boil away Earth's oceans and kill everything on the dried-out surface. This could

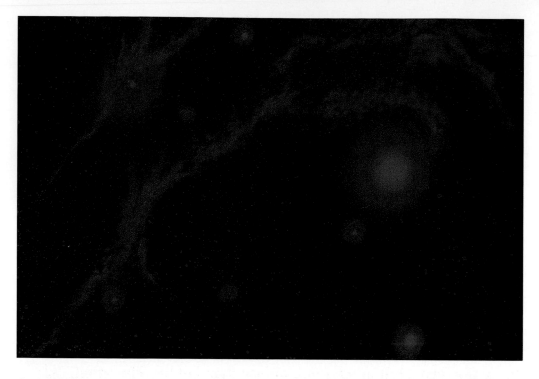

Several billion years from now, the white, yellow, and blue stars that now fill the sky will turn into Red Giants, as shown in this illustration. Among these dying stars will be the Sun.

happen in closer to 1.5 billion years if a changing atmosphere on Earth traps enough heat to speed up the global warming process.

THE DEATH OF THE SUN

When the Sun's core burns out, more hydrogen just outside the core will ignite. This will make the Sun balloon outward. The Sun will then become a Red Giant. It will grow bigger and bigger until it swallows the planet Mercury. It will glow two thousand times as bright as it does now, and all the stone and metal on Earth's surface will melt.

While the outside expands, the Sun's burned-out core will continue to cool and shrink. With its hydrogen fuel gone, the core will be mostly helium. When the core contracts enough, heat from the burning hydrogen shell around it will set off a new round of fusion in the core. This time, helium atoms will fuse to become carbon and oxygen. With helium fusion heating the core, and hydrogen fusion heating the shell, the Sun will become forty-four times hotter than it is today. Around 12.3 billion years after its birth, the helium in the core will be used up. It will then shrink in size, but only temporarily. The helium in outer layers will ignite, causing a series of "helium flashes" that will turn the Sun again into a Red Giant. During each helium flash, the Sun will expand to one hundred times its current size. It will then cool and shrink, until another helium flash occurs. This could happen four to ten times, until the helium fuel is used up.

Without hydrogen or helium fuel for nuclear fusion, the Sun's nuclear furnace will go out. With no internal heat source to battle the Sun's gravity and keep the gases puffed out, the Sun will shrink to about the size of Earth. Leftover heat will make it continue to glow for many years, but much more faintly than before. The small, dim star will then be a White Dwarf. When it finally grows cold and dark, it will become a Black Dwarf.

THE DISTANT FUTURE

What does the fate of the Sun mean for the future of humanity? Any changes in the Sun are too far off to worry about. Human beings have existed for less than 2 million years. We have hundreds of times that long before Earth will become uninhabitable. This should give our descendants plenty of time to find a new place to live.

Until then, manmade threats to our home planet will pose a much more serious danger than any changes in the Sun. If we can keep the environment here on Earth safe and healthy, the Sun will warm us with its life-giving rays for millions and millions of years to come.

GLOSSARY

atmosphere the layer of gas surrounding a planet

atom the smallest particle of a given chemical element, made of a nucleus and surrounding electrons

atomic having to do with atoms

Big Bang a theory of the origin of the universe, in which all matter was created by the giant explosion of a single point in space

charge a quantity of electricity, measured as either positive or negative; a positively charged object pushes away other positively charged objects, but attracts negatively charged objects

current the flow of electricity

cycle a repeating pattern

density a measure of how tightly packed together matter is in a given amount of space

element one of the basic chemicals from which everything else is made

fusion joining together two things into one; nuclear fusion means bonding two atomic nuclei into a new atom

gas a form of matter in which molecules or atoms float freely instead of being connected together, as they are in a solid

gravity the force of attraction between objects; the more massive the object, the stronger the force

magnetic field the space around an electric current in which magnetic forces can be felt

mass a measure of the amount of matter something contains

nebula a giant cloud of gas and dust in space, from which stars and planets form

nuclear having to do with atomic nuclei

nucleus the center of an atom (plural is **nuclei**)

orbit the path an object takes around a larger object in space, such as a planet around the Sun

photon a small unit of light energy

planet a large ball of matter orbiting a star

plasma a mixture of atomic particles that is neither gas, liquid, nor solid

pressure a force that squeezes or compresses something

radiate to send out rays of energy

radiation waves of energy

revolve to travel in an orbit around another object

rotate to turn or spin, like a steering wheel or a globe on a stand

solar having to do with the Sun

Solar System the Sun and everything orbiting it, including planets, moons, asteroids, meteoroids, and comets

star a giant ball of gas with a nuclear reaction in the center that produces light and heat

uninhabitable impossible for people to survive in

volume a measure of the amount of space that something takes up

FIND OUT MORE

BOOKS FOR YOUNG READERS

Asimov, Isaac. *What Makes the Sun Shine?*. Boston: Little Brown, 1971.

Couper, Heather, and Nigel Henbest. *How the Universe Works*. Pleasantville, NY: Reader's Digest, 1994.

Daley, Michael J. *Amazing Sun Fun Activities*. New York: McGraw-Hill, 1997.

Gallant, Roy A. *When the Sun Dies*. New York: Marshall Cavendish Corporation, 1999.

Gardner, Robert. *Science Project Ideas About the Sun*. Springfield, NJ: Enslow Publishers, Inc., 1997.

Vogt, Gregory L. *The Solar System: Facts and Exploration*. New York: Twenty-First Century Books, 1995.

OTHER BOOKS

In doing research for this book, I found the following books especially helpful:

Beatty, J. Kelly, Carolyn Collins Petersen, and Andrew Chaikin, eds. *The New Solar System*. 4th ed. New York: Sky Publishing, 1999.

Booth, Nicholas. *Exploring the Solar System*. New York: Sky Publishing, 1996.

Fire of Life: The Smithsonian Book of the Sun. Washington, DC: Smithsonian Exposition Books, 1981.

Gallant, Roy A. *When the Sun Dies*. New York: Marshall Cavendish Corporation, 1999.

Websites

http://seds.lpl.arizona.edu/nineplanets/nineplanets/sol.html
An introduction to the Sun, including a glossary and a broad selection of links to related sites.

http://www.astro.uva.nl/demo/od95
A virtual tour of the Sun with pictures and video clips of solar activity.

http://solar-center.stanford.edu/folklore/folklore.html
Legends and folktales about the Sun from every corner of the globe.

http://www.spaceweather.com
Detailed information about how the Sun's fluctuations affect Earth, including current conditions and forecasts.

http://www.science.nasa.gov
A searchable collection of news about astronomy from NASA.

http://www.space.com
All the latest astronomy-related news.

http://www.spacekids.com
Fun facts and games about space for kids.

ABOUT THE AUTHOR

Martin Schwabacher has written more than twenty books for children, including *Jupiter* in the **Blastoff!** series. He has also written books about asteroids and meteorites, weird rocks, elephants, and bears. He has contributed to the American Museum of Natural History's exhibitions and websites and has also written for other websites about space. He grew up in Minnesota and lives in New York City with children's book writer Melissa McDaniel and their daughter, Iris.

INDEX

Page numbers for illustrations are in bold.